Biography of a Slave

Biography of a Slave

The Biography of a Slave

Being the Experiences of Rev. Charles Thompson, a Preacher of the United Brethren Church, While a Slave in the South. Together with Startling Occurrences Incidental to Slave Life

LARGE PRINT EDITION

By

Charles Thompson

b. 1833

Biography of a Slave

PREPARED FOR PUBLICATION
BY
HISTORIC PULISHING

All Rights Reserved. No part of this publication may be reproduced, stored in a retrieval system, or transmitted, in any form, or by any means, electronic, mechanical, photocopying, recording, or otherwise, without the prior consent of the publisher.

Biography of a Slave
ISBN: 1946640328

Biography of a Slave

All Rights Reserved
HISTORIC PULISHING
©2017 (Edited Materials)

THE BIOGRAPHY OF A SLAVE

BEING THE EXPERIENCES

OF

Rev. Charles Thompson,

A PREACHER OF THE UNITED BRETHREN

CHURCH,

WHILE A SLAVE IN THE SOUTH.

TOGETHER WITH STARTLING OCCURRENCES

INCIDENTAL TO SLAVE LIFE.

By

Charles Thompson

DAYTON, OHIO:

UNITED BETHREN PUBLISHING HOUSE.

1875.

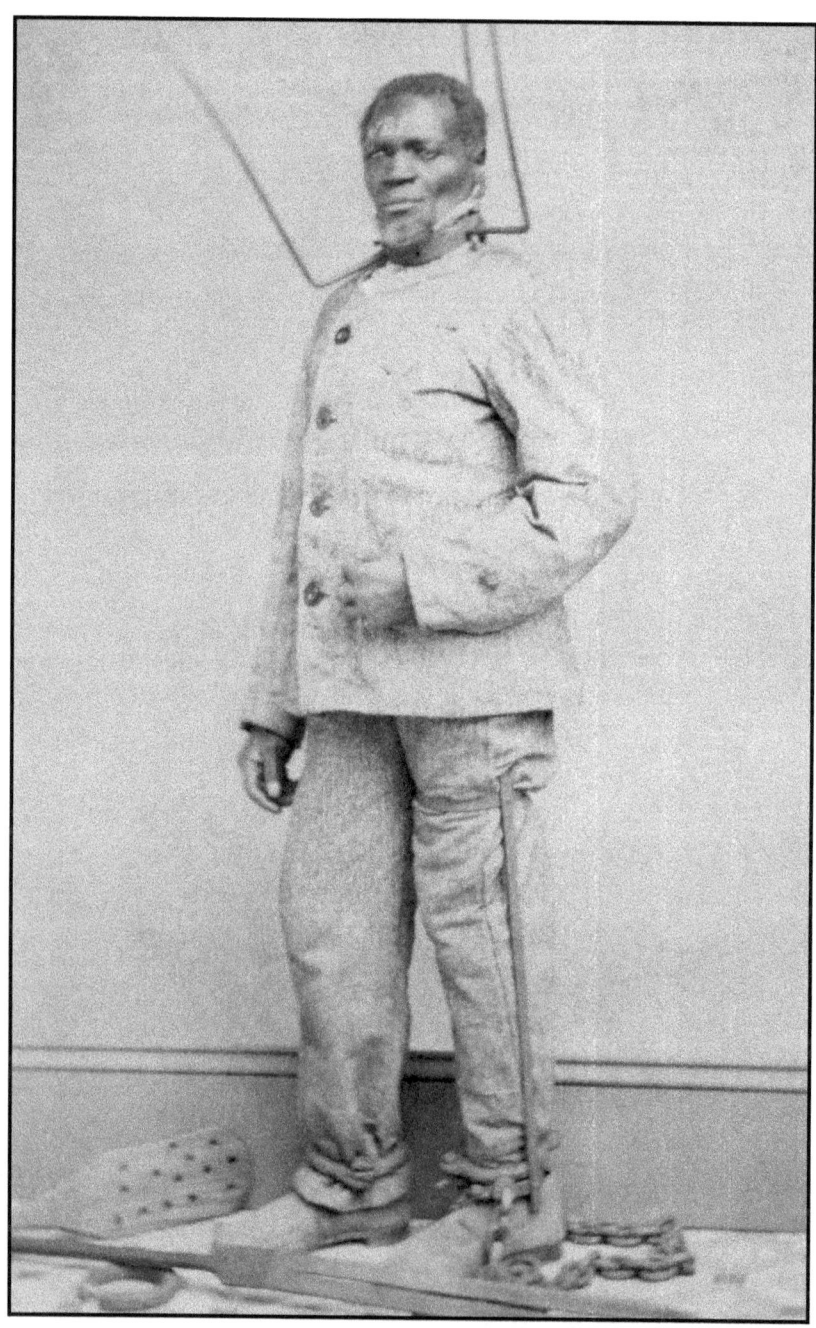

Biography of a Slave

PREFACE.

In publishing this book, I hope to do good not only to my own race, but to all who may read it. I am not a bookmaker, and make no pretensions to literary attainments; and I have made no efforts to create for myself a place in the literary, book-making ranks. I claim for my book truthfulness and honesty of purpose, and upon that basis, it must succeed or fail. The Biography of a Slave is called for by a very large number of my immediate acquaintances, and, I am assured, will meet with such reception as to justify the expense I have incurred in having it printed and bound. To the members of the United Brethren Church, white as well as colored, I look for help in the sale and circulation of my work, yet I am satisfied I will receive commendable patronage from members of all Christian churches everywhere.

The book is written in the narrative style, as being much better suited to the tastes and capacities of my colored readers, and I have used simple and plain English language, discarding the idiomatic and provincial language of the southern slaves and ignorant whites, expecting thereby to help educate the blacks in the use of proper language.

I am indebted to William H. Rhodes, Esq., attorney at law, of Newman, Douglas County, Illinois, for his valuable assistance in the preparation of my manuscript for the printer. He has re-written the whole of it for me, and has otherwise assisted me in the matter of placing the book before the public.

CHARLES THOMPSON.

Newman, Illinois, Aug., 1874.

Biography of a Slave

CONTENTS.

CHAPTER I.

Charles Thompson, born in Atala County, Mississippi--Division of Kirkwood's slaves among his six Children--The writer and his two sisters fall to Mrs. Wilson--The parting between mother and child--Deprived of a fond mother forever--Old Uncle Jack--Wilson buys Uncle Ben from Strucker--Uncle Ben runs away and is hunted with blood-hounds--Two hundred dollars reward. **21**

CHAPTER II.

Not sent to hell by Wilson--Mrs. Wilson protects me, to whom I belong--Sent to school with the children--The school-children teach me to read and write--What came of it--Mount that mule or I'll shoot you--I mounted the mule--A start for the railroad to work--I dismount and take to the woods--I owe allegiance to God and my country only. **41**

CHAPTER III.

Caught, tried, and taken back home to James Wilson--My mistress saves me from being whipped--I go to the railroad and work one month precisely--Go back home--Wilson surprised--Left the railroad at 3 o'clock A. M.--Did not want to disturb Leadbitter's rest--Sent to Memphis with a load of cotton--Afraid of the slave-pens and slave-auction--Start for home--Not sold--Pray, sing, and shout--Get home and ordered to hire myself out. **70**

CHAPTER IV.

Start out on my travels to hunt a new master--Find Mr. Dansley--Hire to him--Thirty dollars per month for my master and five dollars for myself--Wilson astonished--Appointed superintendent of Dansley's farm--

Rules and regulations--Peace and tranquility--My moral labors successful--Prayer and social meetings--Meetings in the woods--Quarrel and fight like very brothers--Time comes to be moved to another field of labor. **93**

CHAPTER V.

James Wilson comes along--Wants me to go with him to Saulsbury, Tennessee, to help build a house for a grocery-store--Takes me along with him--Wilson taken sick--I take care of him--He gets well--I make another attempt to escape from slavery--What came of it. **115**

CHAPTER VI.

Was hired to Mr. Thompson, and adopted his name--Opened regular meetings, and preached on the plantation and other places--Took unto myself a wife--Was purchased by Thompson, duly installed on the plantation, and invested with authority--Various means and plans resorted to by the overseer to degrade me in the eyes of Mr. Thompson--Driven, through persecution, to run away--Return back to my master. **146**

Biography of a Slave

Biography of a Slave

BIOGRAPHY OF A SLAVE.

CHAPTER I.

Charles Thompson, born in Atala County, Mississippi--Division of Kirkwood's Slaves Among his Six Children--The Writer and his Two Sisters Fall to Mrs. Wilson--The Parting Between Mother and Child--Deprived of a Fond Mother Forever--Old Uncle Jack--Wilson Buy's Uncle Ben from Strucker--Uncle Ben Runs Away and is Hunted with Blood-Hounds--Two Hundred Dollars Reward.

I was a slave, and was born in Atala County, Mississippi, near the town of Rockford, on the third day of March, 1833, My father and mother both being slaves, of course my pedigree is not traceable, by me, farther back than my parents. Our family belonged to a man named Kirkwood, who was a large slave-owner. Kirkwood died when I was about nine years old, after which, upon the settlement of the affairs of his estate, the slaves belonging to the estate were divided equally, as to value, among the six heirs. There were about seventy-five slaves to be divided into six lots; and great was the tribulation among the poor blacks when they learned that they were to be separated.

When the division was completed two of my sisters and myself were cast into one lot, my mother into another, and my father into another, and the rest of the family in the other lots. Young and slave as I was, I felt the pang of separation from my loved and revered mother; child that I was I mourned for mother, even before our final separation, as one dead to me forever. So early to be deprived of a fond mother, by the "law," gave me my first view of the curse of slavery. Until this time I did not know what trouble was, but from then until the tocsin of freedom was sounded through the glorious Emancipation Proclamation by the immortal Abraham Lincoln, I passed through hardship after hardship, in quick succession, and many,

many times I have almost seen and tasted death.

I bade farewell to my mother, forever, on this earth. Oh! the pangs of that moment. Even after thirty years have elapsed the scene comes vividly to my memory as I write. A gloomy, dark cloud seemed to pass before my vision, and the very air seemed to still with awfulness. I felt bereaved, forlorn, forsaken, lost. Put yourself in my place; feel what I have felt, and then say, God is just; he will protect the helpless and right the wronged, and you will have some idea of my feelings and the hope that sustained me through long and weary years of servitude. My mother, my poor mother! what must she have suffered. Never will I forget her last words; never will I forget the earnest prayers of that mother begging for her child, and refusing to be comforted. She had fallen to the lot of Mrs. Anderson, and she pleaded with burning tears streaming down her cheeks, "He is my only son, my baby child, my youngest and the only son I have; please let me have him to go with me!"

Anderson spoke roughly to her and told her to hold her peace; but with her arms around me she clung to me and cried the louder, "Let me have my child; if you will let me have my baby you may have all the rest!"

Mothers can realize this situation only, who have parted with children whom they never expected to see again. Imagine parting with your dearest child, never to see it again;

to be thrown into life-servitude in one part of the country and your dear child in the same condition six hundred miles away. Although my mother was black, she had a soul; she had a heart to feel just as you have, and I, her child, was being ruthlessly torn from her by inexorable "law." What would you have done if you had been in her place? She prayed to God for help.

My kind old father consoled and encouraged my mother all he could, and said to her, "Do not be discouraged, for Jesus is your friend; if you lack for knowledge, he will inform you, and if you meet with troubles and trials on your way, cast all your cares on Jesus, and don't forget to pray." The old man spoke these words while praying, shouting, crying, and saying farewell to my mother. He had, in a manner, raised nearly all the colored people on the plantation; so he had a fatherly feeling for all of them. The old man looked down on me, and said, "My child, you are now without a father and will soon be without a mother; but be a good boy, and God will be father and mother to you. If you will put your trust in him and pray to him, he will take you home to heaven when you die, where you can meet your mother there, where parting will be no more. Farewell." I was then taken from my mother, and have not seen or heard of her since--about twenty-nine years ago. Old Uncle Jack, as my father was called by the plantation people, spoke words of comfort to all of us before we were parted.

The lot of human chattels, of which I was one, was taken to their new home on Wilson's plantation, in the same county as the Kirkwood plantation. Wilson told my sisters and myself that our mother and ourselves were about six hundred miles apart.

After I had been in my new home about two years, Wilson bought my uncle Ben from a man named Strucker, who lived in the same neighborhood, but he did not buy uncle Ben's wife. Two years later Wilson moved to another plantation, he owned in Pontotoe County, Mississippi, about one hundred miles distant from his Atala County plantation. Ben not being willing to go so far from his wife, ran away from his master. Wilson, however, left word that if anyone would catch and return Ben to him, he would pay two hundred dollars. This was a bait not to be resisted. The professional slave-hunters, with their blood-hounds, were soon on the track. They failed to get the poor hunted man, though. Ben was a religious, God-fearing man, and placed firm reliance on the help of the Almighty, in his serious trials, and never failed to find help when most needed. He stayed under cover in the woods, in such lurking places as the nature of the country provided, in the day time, and at night would cautiously approach his wife's cabin, when, at an appointed signal, she would let him in and give him such food and care as his condition required. The slaves of the South were united in the one particular of helping each other in such cases as this, and would adopt ingenious telegrams and signals to communicate with each other; and it may well be believed that the inventive genius of the blacks was, as a general thing, equal to all emergencies, and when driven to extremities they were brave to a fault. Ben's wife, in this instance, used the simple device of hanging a certain garment in a particular spot, easily to be seen from Ben's covert, and which denoted that the coast was clear and no danger need be apprehended. The garment and the place of hanging it had to be changed every day, yet the signals thus made were true to the purpose, and saved uncle Ben from capture. Uncle Ben was closely chased by the hounds and inhuman men-hunters; on one occasion so closely that he plunged into a stream and followed the current for more than a mile. Taking to the water threw the hounds off the scent of the track. Before reaching the stream, uncle Ben was so closely pursued that one of the men in the gang shot at him, the bullet passing unpleasantly close to him. His wife heard the hounds and the gunshot. This race for life and liberty was only one of a continued series, and was repeated as often as bloodhounds could find a track to follow. At night Ben was very much fatigued and hungry, and his only hope of getting anything to eat was to reach his wife's cabin. How to do this without being observed, was the question. As well as he was able, about midnight he left his retreat and approached the cabin. It was too dark to see a signal if one had been placed for him in the usual manner. After waiting for some time a bright light shot through the cracks in the cabin for an instant, and was repeated at intervals of two or three minutes, three or four times. This was the night-signal of "all right" agreed upon between uncle Ben and his wife, and was made by placing the usual grease light under a vessel and raising the vessel for a moment at intervals. Ben approached the cabin and gave his signal by rapping on the door three times, and after a short pause three more raps. Thus they had to arrange to meet; the husband to obtain food to sustain life, and the wife to administer to him. On this particular night their meeting was unusually impressive. She had heard the death-hounds, the sound of the gun-shot, and she knew the yelps of the hounds and the shot were intended for Ben, her husband. With no crime laid to him, he was hunted down as a wild beast. Made in God's own image, he is made a slave, a brute, an outcast, and an outlaw because his skin is black. Thus they met, Ben and his wife. After the usual precautions and mutual congratulations they both kneeled before the throne of God and thanked him for their preservation thus far, and throwing themselves upon his goodness and bounty, asked help in their need and safety in the future. Without rising from his knees, Ben, even in the anguish of his heart, consoled his wife, remarking, "that the darkest hour is always just before daylight."

The blacks of the South have their own peculiar moral maxims, applicable to all situations in life, and the slaves not knowing how to read committed such Bible truths as were read to them from time to time. It is true they were generally superstitious in a great degree, as all ignorant persons are; yet their native sense of right led them to adopt the best and most religious principles, dressed in homely "sayings," their circumstances permitted.

Ben dare not stay very long at a time in his wife's cabin, as a strict watch was constantly kept, that the runaway might be apprehended. Bidding his wife farewell, Ben hastened back to one of a number of his hiding-places, there to stay through the day, unless routed out by the bloodhounds. He was fortunate, however, in the help of God, for his safety, and the efforts of the hounds and the hounds' followers were futile.

Finally, Wilson gave up chasing Ben with bloodhounds, and resolved to try a better and more human method. He bought Ben's wife and left her with Strucker, with instructions to send her and Ben to his plantation if Ben was willing for the arrangement. Ben soon got word of how matters stood with reference to himself, and concluded if he could live with his wife on the same plantation that it was the very best he could do, so he acceded to the wishes of Wilson, and was sent with his wife to Wilson.

The happiness of this couple was unbounded when they found they could once more live together as God intended they should, and the poor wife in her great gratitude cried, "God is on our side!" Ben replied that he had told her on one occasion that God was on their side, and that "the darkest hour was just before day."

The usual expression used by the blacks when a runaway returned to his master was that he "had come out of the woods;" that is, he had left his hiding place in the woods and returned to the plantation to work.

When I heard that uncle Ben had come out of the woods, and was coming to live on our plantation, my joy knew no bounds. On the day when he was expected to arrive, I got permission to go out on the road some distance and meet them. Early in the morning, I caught a horse and started. Every wagon I met filled me with hope and fear blended; hope that the wagon contained my uncle and aunt, and fear that it did not. I rode on, on, on, all that day, until my heart was sick with hope deferred. I had received orders before starting that if I did not meet them that day to return home. But I was so far from home, and with straining my eyes to catch a glimpse of my uncle, added to my keen disappointment in not seeing them, made me feel tired, sick, and worn out. So I stopped at a friendly cabin that night, after telling the inmates who I was and what my errand was. Early the next morning I was out, and the anxiety to see my uncle was so great I thought I would ride out the road a short distance in the hope of meeting him, notwithstanding my orders to return home. After traveling about an hour I met the wagon containing uncle Ben and his wife. The joy of that moment to me is inexpressible. Having been deprived of mother and father he was the only relative my sisters and myself could ever have any hopes of seeing again. My heart rejoiced exceedingly. I was, as it were, a new boy entirely, so overcome was I. We all arrived home that same day, and it was a much more pleasant trip than I had taken the day before. On that day it was all anxiety, mixed with hope and fear; to-day it was all joy and thanksgiving, again proving uncle Ben's saying that "the darkest hour is always just before day. My sisters were simply wild with joy when we arrived. They ran out the road to meet, us crying, "There comes uncle Ben; we have one more friend!" We were all comforted and rejoiced to a very great extent, and we felt indeed that we had "one more friend" with us. We were as happy as slaves could be, and spent all the time we could together--uncle Ben, his wife, my sisters, and myself.

But Wilson harbored a grudge toward uncle Ben because he had to buy his wife in order to get him, and had said that if he ever got Ben after he ran away he would whip him to death. He treated Ben very well for the time being, but about a year after he had got him home he began to put his plans into operation for severely punishing him. He was afraid of Ben's prayers. Although Wilson would not have hesitated a moment to have put any plan into execution he may have conceived, under ordinary circumstances, yet praying Ben, while defending himself by appeals to Almighty God was stronger than with carnal weapons in his hands. Wilson proceeded cautiously and laid shares for Ben. Uncle Ben was one of the best hands on the plantation, and religiously performed the labor allotted him truly and persistently. He obeyed his overseer and Wilson in all things pertaining to his manual occupation, and obeyed God to the very best of his ability in this as in everything else. But Wilson wanted to punish Ben, and was determined to do so. He knew that Ben was a faithful slave to labor, and was reliable, yet he wished to break Ben's spirit--his manhood, the God part of him. Wilson did not seem to know that he was not fighting Ben in his scheme of revenge but that he was fighting God in Ben, and that although he punished Ben to the death he would be conquered himself, and more severely punished than he could ever hope to punish Ben. But Wilson was mad, infatuated, and satanically determined. Precautious preparations were made by Wilson to insure success in his revengeful scheme, and after having obtained the aid of several neighbors who were what might be called professional slave-whippers, he deemed his undertaking to punish and conquer Ben fully ripe for execution. Ben being a field hand was busily employed picking cotton, with a prayerful heart, and a watchful eye on Wilson. From Wilson's actions, Ben was sure something was going to occur which would nearly concern him, and having been hunted like a beast he had become suspicious and on his guard all the time. Having a feeling of presentiment, he was uneasy, and, as was usual with him, he kneeled down and asked God to protect him from the machinations of his enemies, and give him heart, courage, and strength to overcome the evil intended him. While praying he was startled by the short of a horse, and on looking around to ascertain the cause of the noise he discovered himself almost surrounded by armed men on horseback. No time to think now; the time for action had arrived. Ben knew at once the flight was for life. Better, however, was death than to be thus hunted and harassed. Bounding through the field he gained a friendly covert, and seemingly by mere chance he eluded his pursuers and the hounds. Ben thanked God for his deliverance. Wilson with his heartless band were again baffled, and with man-hunting and disappointments in his man-chase he became furious. Ben stayed in the woods about four, weeks, and during all this time my sisters, Ben's wife, and myself were kept in close confinement, to keep us from communicating with Ben or rendering him any assistance. Thus all of us had to suffer. But we were only slaves.

Wilson finally took Ben's wife to a man in Oxford, about twenty-five miles distant, and came back circulating the word among the blacks that he had sold her. Wilson had made arrangements at Oxford with some professional slave-hunters to catch Ben if he ever came to see his wife, for which purpose she had been taken there.

After a time Ben was informed that he and his wife had been sold by Wilson to a man in Oxford, and of course believing such to be the fact, he went there to see her, and make arrangements for the future. His wife was told by the man with whom Wilson had left her that he had bought both her and Ben, and wished her to get Ben to "come out of the woods." Laboring under this delusion,

Ben was trapped while in bed for the first time in a month. The cabin was surrounded by armed men, when Ben was overpowered, chained, and put in jail for safe keeping until Wilson should come after him. Living in the woods so long and the harsh treatment he was now receiving wore Ben down considerably; yet, believing that "the darkest hour is just before day," he relied on God's help in his misery.

Wilson came for Ben in due time, and after chaining him securely around the neck he fastened one end of the chain to the rear of his buggy and literally, a part of the time, dragged him to Holly Springs, about thirty miles from Oxford, where he sold him to a man who had the reputation of being the hardest master in the country. Wilson afterwards took Ben's wife home. Thus they were separated,--Ben and his wife,--never to meet again on this earth.

Wilson told me when he got home that he had sent Ben to hell, and that he would send me there too. Infatuated man; he supposed he had done with Ben for the very worst; he thought he had as much power over the souls of his slaves as he had under "the laws" over their bodies. He found, however, in time, that God was with us, and in his good time he delivered us from our bondage and punished our persecutors as they deserved.

CHAPTER II.

Not sent to hell by Wilson--Mrs. Wilson protects me, to whom I belong--Sent to school with the children--The school-children teach me to read and write--What came of it--Mount that male or I'll shoot you--I mounted the mule--A start for the railroad to work--I dismount and take to the woods--I owe allegiance to God and my country only.

The monotonous tedium of routine slave-labor was very often broken by some scene of cruelty to one or another of the poor blacks, either by the master or his overseer; and woe unto the luckless one if the master should happen to be in a good mood to break bones. Although slaves were worth money in the South at that time, yet the ungovernable passions of some if not most masters found free vent in cruelty to their own property--that is, their slaves. This was the case with

Wilson, and no opportunity was missed by him to make a poor black feel the effects of his brutish nature and passions. His wife, on the other hand, made every effort to protect the blacks on the plantation as much as possible. When Wilson threatened to send me to hell, as he had tried to send uncle Ben, Mrs. Wilson came forward in my behalf and saved me from her husband's unwarranted wrath by telling him that she wished "Charles to accompany her children to school and take such care of them as might be required." It was customary in the South for families who owned slaves to send one or more of them with their children when they attended school as waiters, or personal servants, and as I belonged to Mrs. Wilson, being an inherited chattel, Wilson acceded to her demand, and I was sent along with the children when they went to school. I was not allowed to sit with the white children in school, but I "loafed around handy," ready for a call from either of my young mistresses.

The "laws," the enlightened laws of the southern states, prohibited, under heavy penalties, the education of a slave, or even a negro, although free; yet some of us; under very disadvantageous circumstances, learned to read and write.

It has always been a kind of habit with me to "be doing something" all the time, and when not actually employed in some active work I would make use of my time for some good purpose; and while "loafing around" that school-house it occurred to me as being strange that the white children should be compelled to sit and study hour after hour, while us little darkies "loafed around" and did nothing. Why couldn't we lighten our young masters and mistresses of that labor as well as other kinds of labor? I determined that my young mistresses should not be made slaves of by the school-master, but that I would do that work for them, as they were generally so kind to me. So I proposed the matter to them, and they were tremendously pleased; at least they laughed and chatted a great deal about me getting their lessons for them, which so elated me that I could not avoid turning handsprings and somersaults all the way home that evening, my joy being so great at the idea of doing my mistresses the favor of taking such great labor off their hands as getting their lessons. I did not doubt my ability, to perform the work, for I was stout, hearty, and large for my age, and could almost make a full hand in the field. Such was my idea at that time of getting lessons. However, the next day my young mistresses told me the school-master would not allow me to study their lessons for them, but that I might take a book and sit outside of the school-house and study there, but that I must be sure and not let any one see me. Why not? Why should I not study lessons in the school-house for my young mistresses? Because it is against the "law" for slaves to learn to read and write. Well, that is curious. A person, because he is a slave, must not study lessons; must not learn to read and write because it is against the "law." What law?

    My mistress used often to read to the children from a book which told about Jesus, and Mary, and Lazarus, and Peter, and Paul; and how Jesus was our Savior, and shed his precious blood for the redemption of all who believed him and would obey his commands; and how Jesus said, "Suffer little children to come unto me, for of such is the kingdom of heaven." Did the "law" prohibit me from studying lessons out of a book about Jesus, and learning to read about Jesus as my mistress did? When my mistress sent my young mistresses to Jesus wouldn't she send me along with them just the same as she sent me to school with them? I reckon so.

Such was my reasoning; and I determined to assist my young mistresses in getting their lessons, law or no law, let the consequences be what they may.

I received the book and went out from the school-house a short distance, and secured myself from observation in a shady place. I opened the book--a spelling-book it was. Hallo! here's a dog and a cat, and here's a sheep too, and right here in the corner is a yoke--a regular ox-yoke. Well, now, this is nice. So I got my first idea of what a book contained by the pictures in a spelling-book. The print in the book meant something, I was sure, and my mind was employed until recess in endeavors to make out what the print and pictures were intended for. The scholars came out at recess, and my mistresses gave me such instructions as they were able, which gave me a start ahead that enabled me to memorize the first six letters of the alphabet by the time school dismissed for noon.

I began to be deeply interested in "studying lessons," and was soon, after hard study, complete master of the alphabet. I could repeat it forwards and backwards, and could instantly tell the name of any letter pointed out to me. My mistresses seemed to take great pleasure in teaching me, and I was very anxious to learn. I soon found that I could understand in a great measure the instructions the teacher gave to the different scholars, by which I profited. I sat in the back part of the house, behind the scholars, with my young mistress' old book in my hand, and held it so that nobody could see it, and studied constantly day after day, which soon advanced me beyond some of the white children older than myself in learning. I learned to spell and read; and my appetite for knowledge increasing, my young mistress set copies for me, and by the time the school-term was out I could spell, read, and write.

Slaves on large plantations in the South were worked in gangs, under the general supervision of the overseer or slave-owner. The gangs were placed under the immediate supervision of a trusty and intelligent slave, whose duty it was to see that each hand performed his or her allotted task, to weigh cotton during the picking season, and to direct the slaves in their labor, and were called field superintendents or bosses. This was my position on the plantation a short time after school was out for the term.

For the first few days after my term at school as waiter for my young mistresses, I was ordered into the field to pick cotton, but was shortly placed over the hands as "boss" and cotton-weigher. Each picker had a "stint" or daily task to perform; that is, each of them was required to pick so many pounds of cotton, and when in default were unmercifully whipped. I had the cotton of each hand to weigh, three times each day, and had to keep the weights of each hand separate and correctly in my mind and report to Wilson every night. I dare not let Wilson or any of the slaves know that I knew anything about figures or could read or write, for a knowledge of those rudiments of education was considered criminal in a slave. The slaves were nearly always jealous and envious of a "boss" of their own color, and left no pretext untried to bring a "boss" into disrepute with the master and consequent corporal punishment. And should I make a misstatement of the weight of any one hand's cotton, that hand would know it. Therefore at the time I am now writing of I had the weights of about three hundred baskets of cotton to report to Wilson every day. This was hard mind-work for me, but I mastered the situation and escaped supersedure and punishment. I held the position of field-superintendent about nine years, and performed my duties faithfully and honestly, to the satisfaction of my master and the hands under me generally.

Why was I so faithful and dutiful to my slave master? Simply because I was doing my duty to God and acting in obedience to the commands of Christ; for my book taught me to do good and shun evil--to obey the revealed will of God no matter what position I might be placed in. As a slave I loved to do the will of the Master in heaven; as a responsible human being I could do no less.

I improved my knowledge, whenever opportunity occurred, and it was but a short time, comparatively, until I found out for myself, by searching the Scriptures clandestinely, the great truths that Jesus taught. I read, pondered, and began the work of self-regeneration. I read that God required of me to do certain things; that unless I obeyed the commands of Jesus I could expect no help from God. I found that I was commanded to "do," and not stand still and wait for others to "do" for me. The way seemed to open before me plainly and unmistakably, and engraved the command to "do" firmly in my heart, in the simple words, "Do the will of God." I obeyed the commands of our Savior in all the essentials of repentance, baptism, and in everything, and began the real work of my life--of living and being a servant of God and a faithful follower of Jesus Christ. My field of labor was my own heart, which I endeavored to render pure in the sight of God. But a short time elapsed when my work within myself began to bear fruit in my efforts to redeem my fellow-slaves from sin and make them children of God. I labored with them in a spirit of brotherly love, and urged them, in season and out of season, to come to Jesus. My labors were not in vain, for a great many were brought to the altar of prayer through my exertions, and were forgiven.

Wilson found out that I could read and write. During the time of cotton-picking, the last season I was superintendent, a protracted meeting was held in the neighborhood, and my master and mistress attended regularly. The only time I could go was on Sunday, and I looked forward to that day with hope and pleasure. On Saturday evening my master stayed to church, and did not expect to return home until Sunday evening. My report of weights were on my mind, and I became somewhat uneasy about the result if I should attempt to remember them until the following Monday. What to do under the circumstances I did not know; yet I knew that "where there was a will there was a way." I was afraid to set the weights down for fear of detection and punishment. I hesitated and tried to think of some safe way out of the dilemma. I knew if I let the matter rest over Sunday I would not remember the weights, for the reason that my mind was so employed and taken up with the religious revival that was then going on in the neighborhood, in which I was very much interested on my own account and on account of my fellow-slaves. I prayed to God to direct me right. The overseer used a slate on which to set down the weights of cotton, which was hanging in his cabin. I took the slate down, made the entries of weights with the names of the pickers, and hung it up again. During the next day (Sunday) the overseer came home, and found the slate with the entries on it I had made. He was somewhat surprised. When Wilson came home he was duly informed of the fact. I was called, and ordered into the presence. I knew it was unlawful for me to know how to write, and I dreaded the consequences of my rash act, yet I unhesitatingly, and with a courage that surprised me, went to the house.

"Who wrote these names and weights on this slate, Charles?" asked Mr. Wilson.

"I did it, sir," I answered.

"How and when did you learn to write?"

"During the time I attended my young mistresses to school, sir."

Wilson looked at me long and angrily, and remarked that I had kept that fact secret for a long time, and that as I had learned to read and write he could not help it. "But you must remember, Charles," he continued, "that the law is that if any negro shall be found writing, his forefinger shall be cut off at the first joint."

My time had now come for my first punishment, I thought. A day or two after I heard Wilson, while in conversation with the overseer, say, "It will not do to let Charles stay with the rest of the negroes, or he will learn them all to read and write, and then we might as well set them free."

What was to be done with me for my unpardonable crime? All kinds of surmises and speculations entered my mind. What was to be my fate? Belonging to Mrs. Wilson--her property--I was placed in charge of her son James, who employed me at teaming, that is, hauling cotton, lumber, etc.

In this occupation I became pretty well acquainted with the surrounding country and the people, and was very well satisfied with matters generally as they then stood. But I was soon to learn that my young master was only anxious to carry out the plans of his father, and was determined to punish, or, as they pleased to term it, "break me," merely because I was related to Ben--because I was able to read and write as well if not better than James Wilson himself.

I was told one day by James that he had hired me to a man in Pontotoc to work in a livery - stable, and that I must come to his plantation without delay. When I arrived I was informed that instead of going to Pontotoc I should go to the railroad then building through Mississippi, and work for Mr. Leadbitter. I expostulated with my master, and urged him, with all the pleas and arguments at my command, to allow me to remain on the plantation or go to Pontotoc, but to no avail. He whipped out his six-shooter, raving and swearing, and bade me mount one of two mules instanter or he would shoot me on the spot. I mounted the mule.

My reasons for not wanting to go to the railroad to work were good. There was plenty to do on the plantation, and there was no good cause for sending me away. I feared rough usage at the railroad, and rougher associations. I had by this time become the religious teacher of all the well-disposed slaves in the neighborhood, and I was so much interested in my labors that I deemed my great Master's work of too much importance to be driven away from it without a struggle. I was no coward, and was always ready to stand out to the end against all opposition, when my duty as a humble follower of Jesus was in question. Therefore my reluctance to be driven from my place of usefulness. However, I got on the mule and started, in company with a colored man who was going with me to bring the mules back. After traveling four or five miles, and when at a convenient place, I dismounted from the mules and told my companion I was going no farther with him, and that if Wilson wanted any one to go to the railroad to work he might go himself; and I "took to the woods."

This was the first time I ever attempted to escape and gain my freedom. Whether I was right or wrong I shall not say, only I ask you to put yourself in my place as I was then situated, and draw your own conclusions. It is true I had formed dear and near associations, and the old neighborhood had been the scene of my trials and triumphs. My master had been uniformly kind, as much so at least as his disposition would allow, yet I felt, although my skin was black, I was entitled to and deserved freedom to worship God according to the dictates of my own conscience, and to teach others the way to everlasting life. I felt that I was a man made after God's own image, and that no one had any right to a property in me as a mere chattel, all human laws to the contrary notwithstanding. I did not deem that I was a criminal, and that I was escaping from penal servitude; but that I was one of God's children, escaping from a worse than Egyptian bondage. I rightfully owed allegiance to God and my country only. So I run away.

CHAPTER III.

Caught, Tried, and Taken Back Home to James Wilson--My Mistress Saves me from Being Whipped--I go to the Railroad and Work one Month Precisely--Go Back Home--Wilson Surprised--Left the Railroad at 3 o'clock A. M.--Did not Want to Disturb Leadbitter's rest--Sent to Memphis with a Load of Cotton--Afraid of the Slave-pens and Slave-auction--Start for Home--Not Sold--Pray, Sing, and Shout--Get Home and Ordered to Hire myself out.

The peculiar feelings one has who is a "runaway" are indescribable. I felt every bit an outcast, and was frightened by the least noise or the sight of any person, and the yelp of a hound was terror to me. I skulked and hid in the woods all day until night, when I concluded to go to town, get something to eat, and make my arrangements for the future.

When the "boy," who was sent by Wilson with me, returned and repeated to him my words, vengeance was sworn against me, and the hounds were turned loose for immediate chase. I went to the town of Pontotoc, and while there refreshing myself in a cabin I heard hounds whining. That was sufficient to inform me that I was trapped. What to do I did not know, but went to the door with the intention of making my escape, if possible, when I was met by James Wilson and five other persons fully armed. Resistance was useless, the hounds would have caught me before I could have run a hundred yards, even if I could have escaped the bullets. I surrendered, and was securely tied by James Wilson and his gang and taken back to the plantation. Dire threats were made against me, but my mistress, James' mother, saved me again. She informed her son that "Charles belonged to her; that Charles' mother had placed him, under the care of God, in her custody, and that she did not intend to have him beaten."

James insisted on "breaking" me, as he termed it, and finally prevailed on his mother, with promises, that if she would let him deal with me he would "break" me without whipping me. She consented. James came to the cabin where I was tied and chained, and told me that he did not desire to whip me, but that if I did not go to the railroad to work every slave on the plantation would become demoralized, and they would all do as they pleased. His words and manner were very kind and conciliatory, yet I took them for what they were worth, and did not believe him; for he would have whipped me severely if he had dared do so. His reasoning regarding the poor, ignorant slaves on the plantation, however, was to the point. In their ignorance they would suppose that if I could do as I pleased and not be punished, they could do the same; and they would, in all probability, create an insurrection which would result in their own destruction. For their sakes I acceded to James' wishes. He told me that if I would go to the railroad and work for Leadbitter one month, that I might after that time hire myself out to whom I pleased and for as long a time as I pleased.

I was given a letter to Leadbitter, and immediately started on foot for the railroad. When I arrived there I handed the letter to Mr. Leadbitter, who asked me how long I had come to stay with him. I told him one month. He broke the letter open, and after reading it informed me that James Wilson stated in the letter that I was to stay as long as he wanted me. This was a piece of intelligence that learned me that James Wilson would lie, and from that time forward I had no confidence in his truthfulness. I did not know what was best to do, but finally made up my mind to fulfill and make good my promise, and trust to the future to compel James Wilson to perform his. I thought this the right course. I did not deem that I would be justified in breaking my promise because Wilson was unreliable and broke his. I concluded that if Leadbitter kept me longer than one month he would have to be smarter than I gave him credit for being. I asked Leadbitter how many days there were in that month.

I went to work, and kept account of the days. I worked carefully. The time passed slowly and wearily. My associations were of the worst character possible, and my co-laborers were of that lowest class of southern blacks whose ignorance and waywardness render them most of the time more than brutal. I made every effort to do good among them, and endeavored to preach to them on several occasions, but was interrupted and deterred by the whites, who forbade my preaching. I talked to the blacks, however, whenever opportunity occurred, and I hope that my labors for Jesus were not in vain.

The last day of my month came and passed. It was Friday. On Saturday morning, about three o'clock, I started for home, and with rapid walking I reached my destination about two hours after sunrise. When I reached the plantation I "cut across lots," and passed through the field where Wilson was at work with the hands. I approached, unobserved by him, and spoke to him. He looked at me with astonishment, and in surprise asked, "What are you doing here?"

"You told me to stay one month; I done so," I answered.

"Did Mr. Leadbitter know when you left?"

"I do not know, sir," I replied. "I left at three o'clock this morning, and did not think it worthwhile to disturb Mr. Leadbitter's rest."

"Three o'clock!" exclaimed Wilson.

"Yes, sir," I quietly answered.

"You ran away, did you?"

"No, sir, I did not run away. I stayed as long as you required me to stay, when, in obedience to your expressed promises, I came home."

James Wilson made some remark I could no understand, but finally said that as I had come home he had some work for me to do before I could hire myself out. I felt somewhat easy in my mind, and waited to be set to work. But when he afterwards told me he wanted me to take a load of cotton to Memphis, my heart misgave me. I felt sure, in my mind, that I was to be sold from the slave-pens at Memphis. The grand trial time had now come for me, and the teachings of my mother and uncle Ben and uncle Jack before and at our final separation came to me in full force. They taught me, before I could read for myself, that in trouble I should rely implicitly on the help of my Savior, and that I should pray without ceasing. To God I immediately turned for guidance and help, and asked that my every step might be directed by him, and that he should protect me from my enemies and persecutors.

I felt that I was being persecuted for Jesus' sake, for I was promised, time and again, that if I would quit preaching and talking to the slaves on religious subjects, I should be advanced and my life made easy and comfortable. I refused the offers, because my Master's work was of more importance than my ease. I was impressed, deeply, with the great responsibilities resting upon me, and was determined to preach and teach while I had strength and opportunity to do so. I may have been mistaken with regard to the cause of my persecution by the Wilsons, but I think not. I do not really believe that any one is persecuted for Christ's sake in this day and age of the world, in a Christian country, except in the South before the rebellion. I have heard men, and, I am almost ashamed to say, preachers, proclaim that they were persecuted because of their adherence to the cause of Christ, when they were not persecuted at all on any account, except probably on account of some wrong act of their own. Paul and the apostles were persecuted, and early Christians were persecuted, but who ever heard of a citizen of the United States being persecuted because he was a follower of Jesus! But slaves in the South were persecuted and punished severely for preaching the gospel of Christ, not on that very account probably, but because it would teach the slaves obedience to a higher power than the inhuman laws of the southern states as they then existed. Paul was persecuted for preaching the redemption of mankind through the blood of the Savior, by pagans and gentiles. I was persecuted for the same reasons by the slave-owners of the South, and for endeavoring to lead the benighted blacks to Jesus. There seems to be some likeness in the positions of Paul and myself. I felt that was the case, at any rate.

My mind was distressed with the fear that I was being sent to Memphis only to be sold to the highest bidder. After addressing the throne of God for help and deliverance I felt relieved, and determined that, come what would, I would use my best talents and exertions for my heavenly Master wherever I might be. Relieved, I set about making preparations for my trip to Memphis, with a prayerful heart. Two of us were going in company, each with a load of cotton. We started on Monday morning, and traveled along without unusual trouble or delay for three days over hilly and rough roads, when we camped for the night within a mile of Holly Springs, in Mississippi, and about fifty-five miles from home.

It will be remembered that uncle Ben was sold by Wilson to a man who lived in and near Holly Springs. I was anxious to see uncle Ben, if possible, and began making inquiries regarding his whereabouts. A colored man came along the road, driving a team, of whom I inquired. After a little time he said a preacher named Ben Harris lived in a house close by, at the same time pointing to it. Upon further inquiries I learned that Ben had taken another wife. This may seem rather criminal, and may appear to be a clear case of bigamy against uncle Ben; but when it is remembered that masters compelled their slaves to live together as man and wife, without ceremony, for the purpose only of breeding children, and that Ben had no say in the matter, he will be held blameless. The laws of the southern states did not recognize the legal relations of man and wife between slaves, therefore they could not commit the crime of bigamy. If Ben was morally guilty, he was forced into his guilt by law and general custom. I had not seen Ben for about ten years, and was so overjoyed at the prospect of seeing him that I could scarcely wait until night, for I was informed that he would not be at his cabin until night. After attending to my affairs about town I waited until sundown, when I went to the house indicated by my informant. Not being certain that the person who lived in the cabin was my uncle, I necessarily had to make inquiries. A colored woman met me at the door, and answered such questions as I asked, from which I was satisfied that Ben lived here. I informed the woman who I was and that Ben was my uncle, and that I had called, in passing on my way to Memphis, to see him. She cordially invited me to enter the cabin, and told me that Ben was out feeding the horses and would shortly be in. I had to wait but a little while when Ben came in. He supposed me to be some passing stranger, and did not recognize me. After some desultory conversation I told him who I was and how I came to be there. Our meeting, after mutual recognition, was affectionate and cordial. We talked over old times and related our experience since we parted at the Wilson plantation. We kneeled at the family altar, and each poured out his soul's thanksgiving to God for his goodness to us, having, before I left, a season of soul-reviving prayer.

Thus we knelt, uncle Ben, his wife, and I, poor slaves in the chains of bondage, really and earnestly thanking God for the many blessings we received. Strange, was it not? when men and women rolling in wealth and all the luxuries and happiness that wealth could purchase, did not even deign to notice the source from whence all their blessings flowed. They had life and liberty, and were unrestrained in the pursuit of happiness, yet not once did they thank the great Giver of all their good. Then what had we, poor wretches, to thank God for? For everything we enjoyed,--for life, for the blessed plan of salvation, for our senses of seeing, hearing, and feeling, for our hearts with which to love him, for our humanity, for the great gifts of sunshine, rain, regulated seasons, the moon, the stars, the earth, the trees, the brooks, the rivers,--everything truly enjoyable we thanked God for. We thanked him for health and strength to do his work. Then we had a great deal to thank Almighty God for, although slaves. How many of you ever think to thank God for sunshine or for reason? Let me illustrate. A gentleman was passing along the highway, when he was met by a poor maniac, who accosted him, saying, "What do you thank God for?" The gentleman being surprised by the abrupt question did not reply immediately, when the maniac continued, "Then thank God for your reason; mine is gone; I'm mad--a maniac." This was something the gentleman had never thought of before, and it opened to his mind an entirely new source of thankfulness. We are apt to forget that we are not slaves, not blind, deaf, or dumb, and not insane; yet should we lose any one of our five senses we would then know how to be thankful for and appreciate that sense should we regain it. Then thank God for everything, your very existence included. Suppose the sun would stop in his course and not shine on the earth but for one day. What consternation and grief there would be throughout the world! Then suppose that after twenty-four hours the sun should burst upon us in all his refulgence and glorious magnificence. What a shout of joy would greet his appearance, and glad hearts would pour out thanks upon thanks to the great Giver for the needful sunshine. Then let us be thankful for all the great blessings bestowed upon us by our heavenly Father, and serve him with all our hearts, in whatever position in life we may be placed. Uncle Ben and I did then, and we do yet.

After a prolonged conversation and a good and refreshing season of prayer I took my departure for my camp, never expecting to meet my relative again, and never have.

We started next morning on our way to Memphis, and traveled into Memphis, after three days, on a very fine road for the South, known as the state-line road. We drove to the cotton-yard, unloaded, and received the receipts for the cotton, and put up for the night at a wagon-yard. I spent this night in prayer and supplication that God would save me from the slave-pen and the auctioneer's block; and my prayers were responded to in my protection. The next morning we started for home by what was known as the pigeon-roost route, in order to save toll and other expenses.

The weight on my mind was removed, and I felt happy and thankful. I was not sold from the shambles. I prayed, I sung, and I shouted by turns. We arrived at home, and I waited patiently for my next order.

My young master soon informed me, however, that I might hire myself out, if I could find and one that would hire me. Good! God was on my side. With a light heart and truly happy I set about my preparations to hire myself out; and the very first thing I did was to go to my cabin and thank God for his goodness, and ask for his protection and guidance. Always praying? Yes, I was always at it. My heart was big with love to God.

Biography of a Slave

Biography of a Slave

CHAPTER IV.

Start out on my Travels to Hunt a New Master--Find Mr. Dansley--Hire to Him--Thirty Dollars per Month for my Master and Five Dollars for Myself--Wilson Astonished--Appointed Superintendent of Dansley's Farm--Rules and Regulations--Peace and Tranquility--My Moral Labors Successful--Prayer and Social Meetings--Meetings in the Woods--Quarrel and Fight like very Brothers--Time comes to be Moved to Another Field of Labor.

It was customary in the slave states to allow slaves to hire themselves for their masters to such as the slaves themselves desired to work for. Sometimes this arrangement was made to save the master trouble. In my case I was instructed to find a place to work at thirty dollars per month and board, and then to return and report to Wilson, who would then give the necessary permission in writing, which would stand as a contract between him and my employer.

My first object was to find a Christian man to hire to who would allow me to pray and preach on all proper occasions, and who would rather assist me than hinder me in my efforts to make Christians of the blacks. I cared nothing for the manual labor I had to do, if I could only be placed in a position to do my great Master's work. His work was my life-labor. On this particular account I was very careful who I applied to. In a day or two I applied to Mr. Dansley, whose plantation was about eighteen miles from Wilson's, and who had been recommended to me as being the kind of man I was hunting for. Mr. Dansley questioned me closely, and examined me as to my reasons for wanting to hire out, and why my master wished me to hire out when there was plenty of work on his own place for me to do. I confessed frankly that I could read and write, and knew something about figures, and was desirous to serve God and do his work by preaching, and in every other way in my power; that my master was afraid that I would demoralize his other slaves by learning them to read and write and by preaching to them, and in order that I might not do that he wanted me off the plantation; that he could not sell me because I was the property of his wife, and that she would not consent to have me sold out of the family. "If those are faults, as considered by Mr. Wilson, I am very well satisfied that you will perform your part of the contract notwithstanding; yet what Mr. Wilson is pleased to consider faults in you I deem good points in your character and disposition, therefore I will hire you, hoping that your duty to God will include your duty to me under the contract of hire." I told him that was my understanding of my duty to God; that it comprised, in my condition of servitude, my duty to my slave-master. I informed Mr. Dansley that my master, Wilson, wanted thirty dollars per month for my services, and that I wanted five dollars per month for myself, making in all thirty-five dollars per month. He was satisfied to pay that amount, and gave me a letter to carry to Wilson stating that he would hire me at thirty dollars per month, yet he agreed with me that he would pay me, besides, five dollars per month.

When Wilson gave me instructions to hire myself out at not less than thirty dollars per month, he hoped I would fail, from the fact that wages for field-hands were only twenty-five dollars per month; and when I went back with Mr. Dansley's letter so soon, he was somewhat surprised. He would have opened his eyes with wonder if he had known that Dansley was to pay me five dollars per month extra. He gave me a written permission to work for Mr. Dansley as long as Dansley should want me. I immediately went to Dansley's, and stayed with him nine months--nine months of contented time.

I found my new master every way worthy of any confidence I might repose in him. In moderate circumstances, he used prudence and diligence in his business transactions and farm operations. He was one of those kind of men some of which may be found in almost every community--an unassuming, industrious, Christian gentleman.

For his farm-force he hired men, both white and black; and when his work pushed him he would require his cook and house-maid, the only slaves he owned, to assist in the fields. At the time of my commencing to work for him he had white men hired who were worse, if any thing, in their habits of shiftless laziness than the lazy blacks. These whites, whom the negroes usually termed "white trash," were, as a general thing, the most vicious, brutal, thieving, shiftless, and lazy human beings imaginable. They were ignorant in the greatest degree, and would not work so long as they could obtain food to sustain life in any other way. They deemed it an honor to be noticed civilly by a respectable negro, and would fawn and truckle to the behests of anyone who had the courage to command them. Such people can be found in no place except the South. They are a result of the system of slavery and slave-laws, and slave-owners are responsible for their condition. Such were the kind of men I had to work with. These men would quarrel and wrangle among themselves, and would consume time and neglect their work. When the house-servants were at work in the field, they would insult and misuse them in every conceivable manner, and it was with great difficulty that Mr. Dansley could get his work done properly and in season. Knowing I had been a farm-superintendent on Wilson's plantation for a number of years, Mr. Dansley immediately appointed me to the same position on his farm, which accounts for his readiness and willingness to pay me high wages.

This was a new kind of position for me, and it required considerable thought and management for me to get matters properly arranged in my mind. "Bossing" white hands and working with them, so as to make their labors profitable for my employer, was no easy task. The farm-work was carried on somewhat similar to the way in which large farms are worked in the northern states, and it required great prudence and watchful care to avoid waste and save all the crops. I arranged my rules of conduct, hours of labor, etc., for the hands, and submitted them to Mr. Dansley for his approval. Mr. Dansley left the matter entirely with me; and, after trial, I found my rules were not sufficiently stringent, and that if I expected to successfully "carry on" that farm I would have to make rules with penalties attached, the men I had to deal with caring little or nothing for mild, persuasive laws. I therefore drew up the following rules, and presented them to Mr. Dansley, and requested him to make them stipulations in the contracts of hire with his men. He approved them, and acceded to my request.

1. Quarreling and using vulgar and profane language is strictly forbidden on the farm, and any hand or hands violating this rule shall be discharged or corrected, in the discretion of the superintendent.

2. Obedience to the just orders of the superintendent is essential to the profitable conduct of the farm; therefore, disobedience to the orders of the superintendent shall be followed by the discharge of the hand or hands so offending, or his or their correction, in the discretion of the superintendent.

3. Each and every hand hereby binds himself to obey the just orders of the superintendent and the rules herein established, and upon the discharge of any

hand or hands, by the superintendent, one month's wages shall be forfeited.

These rules were signed by the hands, that is, they "made their mark;" but I signed my name, being the only negro hand on the place and the only one who could write.

Peace and tranquillity reigned on that farm thereafter, and better crops were not raised in the county. My whole study and aim was to do right--to be just to my hands and do my duty to my employer. I relied on God's help, and prayerfully asked his guidance in every and all difficulties and emergencies, and my success is attributable to that help which is always given when properly asked for.

The men I had to deal with were more to be pitied than blamed. They were entirely ignorant of any but the most crude principles of right, and were taught from their childhood only such rude notions as prevailed among the ignorant. When I talked to them of Jesus, they seemed astonished. They did not even know that punishment would meet them hereafter for their sins committed in this life, and were puzzled and perplexed with the plan of salvation until after I had repeatedly explained it to them; in fact, I taught them the history of man, from Adam down to the coming of our Savior, and taught them the religion of Jesus. Better-behaved men or better hands were not to be found in the neighborhood after they learned the way to Jesus, and many happy times we did have on that farm at our prayer-meetings and social gatherings. All of us would meet at some convenient place on the farm, every Sabbath-day, and would spend the time profitably, in exhortation and prayer. The master and mistress were always there, and worked with a will in the cause of Christ, and I would exhort and preach to the best of my ability. Sometimes Mr. Dansley would read a chapter from the Bible and comment thereon, and sometimes his wife would read and comment. All of us prayed, and some of the white hands became, in a short time, earnest public prayers. They had found the fount of true happiness, and would drink largely therefrom on all occasions.

Our regular Sunday meetings soon became known in the neighborhood, and the neighbors and their slaves would come and worship with us, until our congregations became so large that Mr. Dansley allowed me to take the hands and clear away a nice place in the woods, and make seats and a stand, where we held our meetings regularly thereafter every Sunday, in the forenoon, afternoon, and at night; besides, we held a social prayer-meeting every Wednesday evening. These meetings were productive of great good to the community and to individuals. In this way I brought men and women to God even while in a condition of slavery, and required to labor six days in the week in the grain and cotton fields. If I, a slave, could accomplish this much, how much should the favored preachers of the country accomplish? This is a hard question to answer, however, and I shall not insist on its consideration, as every preacher cannot be a Lorenzo Dow, a John Smith, or a James Findley.

Among the field hands under me were two brothers, white men, who, when I first took charge of the farm were maliciously wicked toward each other, and were almost constantly quarreling just like brothers (!). Before three months had elapsed, under my kind of treatment, they were praying, acting Christians, and remained so as long as I knew them.

From this time down to the present writing I have been a zealous worker in the

Lord's vineyard, and shall remain in the harness as long as God wills.

Regarding doctrinal points of theology I knew nothing, and my whole stock of theological works could have been carried in a vest pocket, in the shape of one or two tracts which fell in my way, and which I read, studied, and preserved. I had a Bible, and that alone served me as the guide in my ministry, and furnished me with all the arguments necessary to the conversion of sinners and their redemption.

Our congregation at Mr. Dansley's was not organized into a church, and I did not attempt to receive members into the church of Christ. I doubted my authority to do so, and any efforts on my part in that direction would have been immediately stopped by the preachers and members of the white churches. But this did not deter me from preaching and exhorting. I believed firmly that God required of me the labor I performed, and I was so much interested and taken up in my work that I did not stop to consider what the consequences would be to myself. My only consideration was, "Where can I find an opportunity to do good and save souls." I asked no pay for my services as a preacher, and never received any; hence I usually found congregations awaiting me at my appointments made up of all classes, white and black, and from all churches organized in the community. My discourses were sometimes off-hand and sometimes studied. It is true my studied discourses were, in the main, original, and taken wholly from the Bible, yet they were none the less effective, because they were earnest and honest. My language was that of the southern blacks and uneducated whites at the beginning of my labors as an exhorter, but after hard study and training I improved myself greatly in this respect, and gained the reputation of being as correct in my pronunciation of English words as the majority of the white preachers. I am not yet entirely free from dialectic pronunciation, and never expect to be; but I find that this very defect, if so it may be called, adds force to my sermons, and gives them a distinctness not otherwise attainable. Therefore I make use of my very faults to do good.

I had hoped to stay with Mr. Dansley as long as he could find it profitable to hire me; and so far I had been of great use to him. I had placed his whole farm in a good state of repair, and had matured and saved his crops in such a manner that his profits were much larger than they ever were before in any one season. I had the goodwill and confidence of the hands, both white and black, who worked under me, and was an instrument in the hands of God in spreading the religion of Jesus Christ in the neighborhood; consequently I was happy and contented, with plenty of all kinds of work to do. But I had accomplished my mission at this place, and it pleased God to remove me to another field of labor, where the harvest was ripe and ready for the reaper. I never complained; on the contrary, I rejoiced that God was not done with me, and had plenty for me to do. When I had thoroughly worked one field of labor, I deemed my immediate services no longer required, and was glad when removed where more work was to be done in God's moral vineyard. Of course I formed intimate associations in every locality in which I was placed, and was prone to leave them; but I was content to do the will of God in every particular, whether that will was expressed through the slave-laws and James Wilson or otherwise.

I was a slave, and was compelled to labor for the profit of my owner, which I performed diligently and faithfully; I was a child of God, and owed him duty and obedience, which I performed earnestly and constantly. From my slave-owners I expected and received no reward or remuneration; from God I received no pay as I labored, but my great reward is yet to come. I have been a depositor in God's bank, from which I expect to draw largely at the final settlement.

CHAPTER V.

James Wilson Comes Along--Wants me to go with Him to Saulsbury, Tennessee, to Help Build a House for a Grocery-Store--Takes me Along with Him--Wilson Taken Sick--I Take Care of Him--He gets Well--I make another Attempt to Escape from Slavery--What Came of it.

One day James Wilson came to Mr. Dansley's, and said he had come for me to go with him to Saulsbury, Tennessee, where he was going to start a grocery, and that he wished my assistance in erecting a building therefor. He informed me, at the same time, that as soon as the building was finished, I might return to Mr. Dansley and stay with him as long as he wanted me. He had another colored man with him, and desired to go right away. All I had to do was to obey, so without further ado I bade farewell to the people of the plantation, and went with Wilson. The parting made me feel sad, for a time.

The word grocery, as applied in the South, has a far different meaning than that intended in the North. A grocery in the South is a place where whisky and other intoxicating beverages are sold, and, as a general thing, at these places the planters and others congregate to drink, carouse, gamble, quarrel, and fight. This was the kind of grocery James Wilson was going to start in Saulsbury, and the thought of aiding even under protest and unwillingly in the establishment of one of these hells caused me much anxiety. I made every effort to get relieved from this odious work, but without avail.

We immediately began the erection of the grocery-building, on our arrival at Saulsbury, and made good progress for a while. The boards we used in the building had to be sawed by us two slaves with a whipsaw. We dug a deep trench in the ground, and laid the log to be sawed into boards lengthwise over the trench, and one of us would stand in the trench under the log and thee other on top of the log. In this way we worked, day after day, until we had a sufficient number of boards to accommodate our wants.

The Almighty, it seemed to me, interfered with our work. James Wilson was taken down very sick in the midst of our efforts to create this additional devil's den, and was totally unable to leave his bed. I had to take care of him, and the work on the grocery-house was necessarily stopped. As soon as he was able to be moved I took him to the Sulphur Springs, not many miles away, and nursed him carefully and attentively until he was able to be about again.

This sickness of Wilson I deemed a warning to him, and endeavored to impress as much on his mind; but I was cursed and reviled for my pains. I availed myself of every opportunity to dissuade him from his evil purpose, but failed. He was determined to start a grocery, and start a grocery he would and did. I cleared my skirts and conscience in the business, however, as far as I could under the circumstances; yet a "still small voice" seemed to whisper to me that I was doing very wicked and sinful acts in helping to further the grocery iniquity. I was, in a manner, forced to work, yet I was uneasy and troubled in my mind. Others may think I was blameless; that I was a slave and not accountable for acts my master commanded me to do. This seemed very specious reasoning, but still I felt guilty, and sent fervent and prayerful petitions to the throne of grace for forgiveness and fortitude to withstand temptation, which enable me to do the will of my great Master regardless of the consequences that might ensue to me from the effects of Wilson's wrath or resentment.

We finished the building in about two months from the time we first went to Salisbury, and prepared to return home.

It was here that I first saw a complete railroad and a locomotive with a train of cars. My fellow-slave, on hearing the whistle of the locomotive for the first time, was very much frightened, and jumped over the log he was hewing, with the exclamation, "Good God! what is that?" and started to run. I stopped him, and, explaining to him what the loud, shrill shriek meant, quieted his fears. We both went to the depot and examined the locomotive and cars with great curiosity and interest.

James Wilson, being still weak with his late sickness, was compelled to ride in the wagon he had brought from home, and I rode his saddle-horse. On the way, Wilson informed me that I was to attend the grocery at Salisbury, and that he expected me to make money out of the concern. My very soul revolted at the bare idea of being a whisky-vender, and my immediate determination was not to be one. My mind was made up to "take to the woods" on the first favorable opportunity. I said nothing, however, but kept my own counsel.

We traveled slowly, by reason of the master's sickness; and when we stopped for the night I found that the saddle I had been riding had hurt the horse's back. Wilson was furious, and swore he would take as much hide from my back when we got home as the saddle had taken from the horse's buck.

The next day after leaving Salisbury we arrived at Mr. Dansley's. In conversation, I heard Wilson tell Mr. Dansley that he intended to take me home with him.

I claimed the fulfillment of his promise from Wilson, and asked him if he was not going to let me work for Mr. Dausley, according to agreement. This so enraged Wilson that he pulled out his six-shooter, and exclaimed:

"Mount that horse, you--black rascal!"

I did so.

Fearful that the horse's back would become incurably sore if I rode him with his back in the condition it was, I suggested that the horse had better be led. Wilson therefore ordered me into the wagon to drive the team, and required Havely, my fellow-slave, to walk,--intending we should take turns. After awhile Havely exchanged places with me, and while walking along in rear of the wagon it occurred to me that this would be as favorable an opportunity as I would soon again get for making my escape from Wilson and slavery.

I "took to the woods" without attracting the attention of either Wilson or Havely, and made good my escape, for the time at least.

I made my way back to Mr. Dansley's and told him my reasons for endeavoring to effect my escape from slavery, and that the immediate cause of my present attempt was to keep myself clear of the accursed sin of whisky-selling. My motives were applauded, but my judgment was condemned.

How could I ever expect to escape to a country where I could be a free man? Even should I escape to the northern states the fugitive slave law, which was then in full force, would remand me back to slavery, and it was a long, tedious, and perilous journey to Canada. I was going to make the attempt at any rate.

It was agreed between us that Mr. Dansley should buy me of Wilson if he could, and that I should stay and work for him at the rate of thirty-five dollars per month until I had re-imbursed Mr. Dansley, when I should have my freedom papers. It would have required about four years for me to pay for myself at those rates, as Wilson "priced" me at sixteen hundred dollars.

The negotiations for my purchase by Mr. Dansley failed, and I was left to my exertions to get to Canada the best way I could. I was secreted during this time about Dansley's farm, and was aroused to a sense of my condition one day by reading a hand-bill which was posted on a tree on the road close to Mr. Dansley's house, of which the following is a copy:

"ONE HUNDRED DOLLARS REWARD!"

"Charles, a slave, has disappeared from the plantation of the undersigned, in Pontotoc County. The above reward will be given for his apprehension and return to me alive.

"JAMES WILSON."

This settled the matter. The reward was soon known over the whole country, and every slave-hunter was on the chase to gain the reward. I "laid close" and waited to escape from that part of the country, so that I might not compromise Mr. Dansley. He was already under surveillance by slave-owners, and was in danger of being driven from the country; in fact, threats of lynching had been made against him.

The last day I was there I lay hid in some cotton-pens, close to the house, when two men came on the hunt of me. They had their bloodhounds with them, and demanded permission of Dansley to search his house. The permission was granted, when the men began the search. I could see and hear all that was going on, and trembled for my safety. I put myself on the mercy of the Almighty and resigned myself entirely into his hands. The search was made all over the premises, including the cotton-pens in which I was hid; but God was on my side, and I was saved from their clutches. I earnestly thanked God for my deliverance on this occasion.

As soon as dark came I emerged from my hiding-place, and, after being supplied with what provisions I could conveniently carry, I bid good-by to Christian Dansley and his family, and started on my perilous journey to the free states and Canada.

My progress was necessarily slow and wearisome, being compelled to travel altogether at night. The first point I designed making on my journey was Memphis, where I hoped to find means of escape to Illinois.

I had plenty of time for meditation and prayer, and my thoughts were naturally concentrated on my deplorable condition all the time. My past life came up in review before me, and while sorrowfully wandering through the woods I would compare myself to persecuted Christians in the days of the apostles and the early evangelists. The blessed Savior was persecuted in his very infancy and had to be hid by his parents. They had to flee for life; I was fleeing for liberty. What had I to complain of? Jesus was with me and would protect me. God had delivered him from the very tomb of death; why need I fear? With these reflections in my mind I would feel revived and refreshed with the consolation that while there was life in me there was hope for me. The words of the poet came to my memory, wherein he says:

> "Neither will he upbraid you,
> Though often your request;
> He'll give you grace to conquer,
> And take you home to rest."

The consolation and help I received from my meditations sustained me through all my trials and hardships, and I plodded my weary way along with God in my heart and bright hopes for the future. I knew if I drew nigh unto God he would draw nigh unto me; and that if I would let the word of Christ dwell in me I would be rich in all wisdom. Yet I was aware I should suffer persecution if I lived godly in Jesus Christ; therefore I determined to continue in the things, which I had learned.

On Sunday night I arrived at Holly Springs. Uncle Ben lived there, and I was anxious to see him and obtain through his assistance, if possible, rest and food. I had proceeded only a little way toward his house when I met a colored man and began conversation with him. I learned that the reward Wilson had offered for me had arrived at Holly Springs before me, and that persons were on the lookout for me. The colored man seemed to have a suspicion that I was a runaway, and was disposed to aid me all in his power. To keep out of the way of slave-hunters was my object, and I knew that the contemplated visit to Uncle Ben was fraught with too much danger to be further thought of.

Fearful that the negro would betray me, yet feeling somewhat safe for the present, I sat down to think and rest myself. I knew that if I was caught Wilson would flay me, as he had threatened to do, for making his saddle-horse's back sore, but that if I could once get through to Memphis I would be enabled, through the assistance of friends, to make my way North. Yet I wanted to see Uncle Ben again, and tried to hit upon some plan to accomplish that object; but I failed, and started on the road again.

After traveling a short time I came to a house by the roadside. The kitchen stood about twenty yards from the main building, and had a window in the back part of it. I was very hungry, and debated in my mind as to the manner in which I should proceed to obtain food. To ask for it was too risky, and I was fearful that if I was seen by any of the persons about the house I would be apprehended and put in the nearest jail as a runaway. Looking in at the window I saw a colored woman; and on a table a meal was prepared, which, it seemed, was being held in readiness for the arrival of someone. I waited patiently, hoping the colored woman would leave the kitchen for some purpose; but she sat quietly waiting.

After a while the master and mistress arrived, it seems, from a visit. Shortly the mistress of the house came in and ordered the supper. Fortunately for me the supper was to be carried into the "big house," and the cook, taking her hands full of things, left the kitchen and went into the house. I immediately sprung through the window, promiscuously emptied the meat and bread into my sack, and left the kitchen the same way before the return of the cook, just in time to escape detection.

I crouched in the shade of the cabin fearing to move, when I heard the cook exclaim:

"Good gracious! someone hab tuk and turned in an' tuk all de bread an' meat."

Her cries brought the household to the kitchen, and during the racket I made my escape to the road and a more peaceful neighborhood. I walked briskly for a couple of miles, when I stopped and satisfied my ravenous hunger.

This was my first theft of something to eat. Before this, I had been fortunate enough to obtain supplies of food from friendly slaves, but for the twenty-four hours previous to my raid on the kitchen I had eaten nothing.

I make no excuse for this immoral act, and ask no one to say I did right. I only did what perhaps anyone else, under the same circumstances, would have done. I was too weak from hunger and other causes to withstand the temptation of obtaining the food as I did. As soon as my appetite was satisfied, however, my sin rose up before me in all its enormity; I felt distressed; and it came vividly in my mind, "In that Christ hath suffered, being tempted, he is able to succor them that are tempted." Oh, what had I done! I had lost God's help in this my hour of trial. I prayed for forgiveness, and asked God to direct and protect me. Yet I felt uneasy and depressed,--not that my faith in Jesus was any the less, but that my sin would bring its own punishment.

"There is many a pang to pursue me;
They may crush, but they shall not contemn--
They may torture, but shall not subdue me,--
of God I think--not of them."

    About daylight I reached a forest in which I could conceal myself during the day. I slept soundly, being undisturbed, until dark, when I proceeded onward. While traveling that night I was compelled to pass a large plantation. I was afraid some white person would see me, therefore I avoided everyone,--not being able to distinguish, in the dark, a white from a black person. However, about daylight I met a colored boy, who procured some food for me and directed me to a cotton-pen close by, where I could hide and sleep during the day. When night came--it was Thursday night--I crawled out of the pen and started for another night's walk. I made very good time that night, and walked to within nine miles of Memphis. I was afraid to go on into Memphis in the daytime, consequently I slept in the woods that day without anything to eat, my supply of food being exhausted.

I was very much exhausted, and suffered greatly from hunger. When night came I started again. After proceeding on my way about two miles I came to the village of Mt. Pleasant, where I thought to obtain something to eat. I had passed nearly through the village without seeing any one; but finally I saw a man who I mistook for a colored man. I accosted him, when, to my chagrin and disappointment, he was a white man. I felt that I had already betrayed myself; and through my fright and want of steadiness I was again in bonds.

The man asked me numerous and various questions, as to where I came from, where I was going, who I belonged to, etc.

I again sinned, and paid the penalty. I lied to the man. I told him I belonged to a man by the name of Potts, and that I was going to his plantation.

Quite a number of persons soon gathered around me, and by repeated questions entrapped me. Inquiries were made as to the health of Mr. Potts' family, and of Mr. Potts in particular. I stated that the family were well and that Mr. Potts was as well as usual.

It turned out that several of the persons present knew the Potts family, and that Mr. Potts had died two months previously.

I was immediately arrested and placed in a secure place, tied and chained to the floor.

Thus sin brought me into trouble. Had I trusted to God and not been in too great haste to get something to eat, he would have helped me. My weakness made me forget that I should not lie to anyone, seeing that I had put off the old man with his deeds. In my great need of strengthening food, Christ would have succored me had I not forgotten to pray to him and ask his help, for "a man can receive nothing except it be given him from heaven."

In nearly all the villages of the South, and on most of the large plantations, were slave-jails, where runaway and refractory slaves were incarcerated. These jails were usually a double pen, the inside pen being covered with a roof, and the top of the outside pen being covered with sharp iron spikes. Between the pens one or more savage dogs were usually kept. This was the kind of place I was now placed in.

Hungry, worn out with my journey, and nearly naked, I soon fell asleep from sheer exhaustion and slept soundly until morning.

After I had eaten my breakfast I was taken out of jail at Mt. Pleasant and started back to Holly Springs, well ironed and guarded, where I was recognized as Wilson's slave. Wilson was notified of my apprehension. After laying in the jail at Holly Springs about three weeks Wilson came for me. I had made several attempts in that time to escape, but did not succeed.

I was ironed and compelled to walk, which, in my exhausted state, was too much for me, and I was taken violently sick on the road, when Wilson procured a conveyance and hauled me the balance of the way home. A physician was immediately summoned, who ordered my shackles removed.

After the irons were removed I regained my spirits, and entertained hopes of being able to make another attempt to regain my liberty. I was very sick for several days.

About two o'clock on the last morning I stayed there I awoke and felt fresh, and found that my strength had in a great measure returned. Upon looking around the moonlit room I found that I was alone. To escape was my very first intention. Getting out of bed I examined the window to the cabin, when I found I could raise it easily. I gathered what clothes I could find, as well as a blanket from the bed, and climbing through the window made my escape unobserved. I did not stop to put on my clothes until I had got two or three miles from the plantation.

I stayed in the woods about three weeks, when I returned to my master and asked his forgiveness, and promised that I would never run away again. I was forgiven.

During my three weeks' starving and hiding in the woods I had ample time for reflection and thought. Prayerfully I considered my situation and asked God's help to direct me. I came to the conclusion that I was entirely wrong in my course. God, for his own good purpose, had placed me in bondage, and in his good time he would relieve me either by death or emancipation. My hardships, I felt, were by reason of my disobedience to God's will. Although I was a slave God had given me my task in his vineyard as a slave, and I should have fronted the wrath of my master, Wilson, rather than that of God. I felt that I was doing wrong, and after prayerful consideration I determined to do right, and go back to the plantation and patiently await God's time to set me free.

Wilson received me as kindly as his nature would permit, and treated me as he did the other slaves and as if I had never been disobedient to him and ran away. I felt better, and knew then that I was right in the sight of my heavenly Father. My views underwent a change for the better while I was an outcast in the woods, and after that I was better fitted to do my allotted work for God.

CHAPTER VI.

Was hired to Mr. Thompson, and adopted his name--Opened regular meetings, and preached on the plantation and other places--Took unto myself a wife--Was purchased by Thompson, duly installed on the plantation, and invested with authority--Various means and plans resorted to by the overseer to degrade me in the eyes of Mr. Thompson--Driven, through persecution, to run away--Returned back to my master.

A short time after I came in from the woods Wilson determined to hire me to a man named Thompson, who lived about twenty miles away. I made no objection, and was duly hired for the term of three years.

I adopted the name "Thompson," from my new master, which I have since retained.

The slaves of the South are usually named like brutes, with only one name for a designation, and it became customary among the slaves to adopt the surname of their masters. I had never adopted the name of Wilson, because I disliked the man; but as soon as I was hired to Mr. Thompson, I took his name, therefore I was henceforth known as Charles Thompson. The adoption of a name by myself may appear strange to a great many of my readers, yet when it comes to be considered that I was a human chattel, with no rights or privileges of American citizenship, and that I was without a name, except simply "Charles," no surprise will be felt.

I labored faithfully and honestly for Mr. Thompson during my term of service, and endeavored in all things to do my duty. I made such efforts as I could to bring the slaves on the plantation to Jesus, and inaugurated regular and stated meetings. I preached and exhorted on the plantation and at other places where I could gather the negroes to hear me; and I felt that I was the means in God's hands of redeeming precious souls. In these meetings, I had helpers from among the most intelligent of the slaves, and made such progress that at all our meetings we would have a number of God-fearing whites to pray with us.

During my term of hired service with Mr. Thompson, I married a colored girl and added the responsibilities of a husband to my various cares.

The marriage of slaves was a more formality among themselves, there being nothing legal, recording to the laws of the southern states, about the ceremony or marriage contract. The slaves cohabited together in most instances with the express or implied consent of their masters; and as the masters did not regard the marriage of their slaves as anything, wives and husbands were constantly in danger of being separated forever.

But the slaves themselves instituted a ceremony, which they considered morally binding, as far as they were concerned; and the slave-owners deemed it prudent to gratify their slaves by a recognition, in some degree, of the marital relations that might exist among them. Therefore, a certain set of rules came into operation, by general consent, governing the visits of the husband to the wife when owned by different masters. When the wife of a slave lived not more than five miles from his master he could visit her once a week: when she lived not more than ten miles away, he could go to see her once in two weeks; and when she lived twenty or more miles away he could go to see her only once in two months.

At the expiration of my term of service I was loth to leave my wife at Thompson's, and go back to Wilson's, and strenuously objected, knowing that I could get to see her only once in two months.

Wilson having learned that I was not desirous of returning to him, wrote to Mr. Thompson to send me home as soon as the last day of my service expired; but Mr. Thompson was desirous of retaining me, and made efforts to that effect. He sent me to Wilson to learn the price set for me. I arrived in due time, when Wilson informed me that he would sell me to Thompson, but that he would not take less than twelve hundred dollars, cash.

The proposition did not seem to please Thompson, but after a time he concluded to buy me, and sent his son to Wilson with the purchase money. The purchase at that particular time was lucky for me, as Wilson had written Thompson a very abusive letter and it was received by Mr. Thompson on the evening of the day on which his son went to Wilson's to buy me. The bargain was made, however, and I was duly transferred to my new master by delivery and a bill of sale. The personal matter between Wilson and Thompson soon blew over and I was duly installed on the plantation as one of the chattel fixtures.

I seemed to take a new lease of life from this time, and determined, if possible, to profit by former experiences and shun every appearance of ill-nature and evil intentions, and to gain the confidence of my new master, that I might better do the work of my heavenly Master. All nature seemed lovely to me, and I was happy in doing my duty and obliging the will of God.

I was invested with authority on the plantation by Mr. Thompson, and was required to keep an eye on the overseer, and to report any enormities that might be committed by him.

Mr. Thompson was a wealthy planter and kept a general overseer, besides the usual field bosses; yet there were other slaves on the plantation who had the confidence of the master and were put at such service as required intelligence and integrity.

The position in which I was now placed was difficult and onerous; but I did my duty to the very best of my ability, and satisfactorily to my master. The overseer soon found out that I was his overseer; and he used every means, and various plans, to drive me to do something that would degrade me in the eyes of Mr. Thompson. It was only by reason of the greatest forbearance and the very closest attention to my duties that I escaped his machinations; and by attending to everything with the most scrupulous care he could find no fault with me, that had truth for its foundation. But the constant and pertinacious maliciousness of the overseer, and my own weakness, eventually brought me to grief.

As a rule, when a bad and wicked man undertakes any species of devilishness he generally prevails, for a time, and is apparently successful in his schemes; and should he meet with failure at the onset his want of success only maddens him to greater exertions and more persistent efforts. Being urged by the devil, and the devil being a hard driver, he either rushes to his own destruction or destroys the happiness or lives of others. Thus I was placed in the crucible for further refinement and regeneration. My humanity gave way for some time; but God was with me, and in the end I prevailed. The overseer's name was Hines, and he belonged to that class of southern whites who are noted for their ignorance and brutality. He could read and write a little,--just enough to make out a negro's pass or a receipt for money paid on account of his employer. In this respect I was far in advance of him, of which my master was aware, and which was one of the causes of Hines' excessive hatred of me, and of his great desire to "put me down and make me know my place," as he termed it. He was very irreligious, and entirely wanting in every attribute of a Christian. He was also what in the South is termed a "bully"--that is, he was free to use his pistols on the slightest occasion, when among his equals, but when in the presence of his superiors he was a cringing sycophant and coward. He was a real coward, at best, in all places. He did not want me on the plantation; and he was determined that he would so harass me that I would become as reckless and devilish as himself, and thereby compel my master to send me to a slave-market to be sold.

Hines concocted various tales and reported them to Mr. Thompson, relating to my alleged insubordination, laziness, refusal to work, etc., but all to no effect. Finally he told my master that I was so disobedient that the rest of the slaves were affected by my conduct, and that I would ruin all the slaves on the plantation unless severe means were used to conquer me.

My master informed Hines, after hearing his story, that Jack, a fellow-servant of mine in my younger days, had killed Prince, another fellow-servant, on Wilson's plantation, several years before; that I might be imbued with the same spirit; and that if he undertook to chastise me he might meet with the same fate of Prince.

This murder occurred after I had been sold by Wilson to Thompson, but being permitted to return to Wilson's plantation once a year to visit and preach to my old flock, I learned the facts regarding the matter.

Jack belonged to a neighbor of Wilson's by the name of Scott, and having done something displeasing to Scott he wished to tie him up and whip him. Jack refused to be whipped by Scott or anyone else, when Prince was called upon by his master (Scott) to help him secure Jack. Prince was reluctant, but was commanded two or three times to take hold of Jack and hold him. Jack told him not to approach him at the peril of his life; but not heeding Jack's warning he made the effort to tie Jack, when he was stabbed to the heart with a knife in Jack's hand, and expired almost instantly. Jack made his escape for a short time, but was captured and immediately hanged without a trial or an opportunity to make any defense. Jack was captured in a corncrib on Wilson's plantation, which made Thompson suppose the murder had been committed there.

This recital, which was made in substance to Hines by my master, cowed the overseer considerably, and a house-servant who was present during the conversation afterwards told me that Hines' face turned white as a sheet, and he trembled like a leaf.

My master knew his overseer was a coward, and that if he could work upon his fears by supposing me to be too high-spirited to stand a whipping, he would probably save me from Hines' malice, and keep the overseer to his work. Good overseers were hard to get in the South. An intelligent Christian man would not have such a position under any circumstances, and the very best of the "poor white trash" who would, were unreliable and brutish; therefore Mr. Thompson had to do the very best he could under the circumstances. He did not believe

Hines; yet he had to humor him, in a measure.

After a few days Hines reported to Mr. Thompson that he had heard me say that I would never be whipped by him or any other overseer on the plantation, as long as I had life to resist, which was a most malicious falsehood. What I did tell Hines was, that I would so conduct myself and so perform my work that he nor any other overseer on the plantation should never have cause to chastise me.

The falsehood inflamed my master, and in his wrath he told Hines to whip me for the first offense I might commit, or kill me in the attempt.

Armed with this instruction, Hines was in high glee; yet he dare not attempt anything without first laying well his plans and making sure of sufficient force to carry them out. The next morning he charged me to pick six hundred pounds of cotton and deliver it at the weighing-house at night, under penalty, for a failure, of one hundred lashes on my bare back with a rawhide.

This would not have been an extraordinary task in good cotton; but where we had to work that day the cotton was poor, and in that field the crop was not more than half a one. However, I worked hard against fate all day, and prayed to Almighty God to help me in my hour of need, and keep me steadfast. I knew I was to be punished not for any fault or misdoing, but simply to gratify a brute in human shape, and my inferior in intellect, morality, and physical strength. The burden was hard to bear, yet I prayed for strength to bear it. When called from the field to the weighing-house I was kept waiting until all the other slaves had their cotton weighed. When mine was weighed I was told by Hines that I had only picked four hundred pounds. I verily believed this to be untrue, and felt convinced that I had picked at least five hundred pounds, for I was one of the best, if not the best, cotton-pickers in the country; and I had labored faithfully and rapidly all day, and did not lose a minute's time, unnecessarily.

Hines turned to me and said, Go to your quarters; I will settle with you in the morning.

Now began new trials. My duty and my Christianity instructed me to face the undeserved and unjust punishment manfully. The devil and my human nature told me to run away. I became weak. The fear of the disgrace of a whipping was too much for me, and I succumbed to the evil one.

I made such arrangements as I could, and concealed myself on the plantation, before daylight the next morning, so that I could take an early start in the night and travel behind my pursuers instead of before them. My wife knew of my hiding-place, and when night came she sought me and reported what had been done for my capture.

Hines seemed, she said, to be more cheerful than usual in the morning when he found I was gone, and hastened to report the good news, as he thought, to Mr. Thompson. After some conversation between them it was determined by my master to obtain the services of a professional slave-hunter, and follow me with hounds. The slave-hunter was sent for and came with his pack of dogs that same day about noon. The hunt was immediately begun, and the country was then being scoured in all directions for my tracks.

This information put me on my guard, and gave me time to consider what direction I had better take in my flight. I had provide myself a preparation called "smut" among the negroes, which, when spread thinly on the soles of the shoes or feet, destroyed that peculiar scent by which blood-hounds are enabled to follow the trail of a man or a beast. After bidding my wife farewell I smeared my shoes with "smut" and started in the direction of the hills, beyond which was a large swamp, the refuge of many a poor runaway.

On my way I had to pass through innumerable thickets of underbrush and briers, and by reason thereof I tore my already much-worn clothes almost into shreds, and lacerated my flesh severely, especially on my arms and legs. I arrived in the swamp, however, without being followed by the dogs, and while proceeding slowly and dejectedly along, my steps were suddenly stopped by a fierce and loud growl. I was frightened, to be sure, yet I knew scarcely what to do. The growl proceeded from a bear, I felt fully assured, for bears roamed through the hills and swamps of Mississippi. But with presence of mind I retreated slowly from the presence of Mr. and Mrs. Bruin, and not being followed by the bears my fears on that score were removed.

About this time it began to rain; and the night was one of those black, foreboding nights that novelists love so well to depict in their descriptions of storms. The lightning flashed with a vividness that lighted up the dismal swamps with a weird and horrible brightness; the thunder rolled peal upon peal, making to me a pandemonium, real and feeling; the pitiless rain pelted me unmercifully and constantly, with that persistence that made it almost unendurable to me. I sat down at the root of a large tree, not to shelter myself from the rain but to protect myself from the attack of any wild animal that should approach me. There I sat the rest of the long night, unfriended, alone, forsaken,--a hunted outcast.

"Man's inhumanity to man
Makes countless thousands mourn."

The condition in which I was now placed rendered me indeed a pitiable object. I waited and longed for morning to come; but the long, slow minutes passed lazily along without regard to my sufferings or wishes. After a long time, to me, I heard a rooster crow, and the welcome sound brought me to my feet in an instant. I started in the direction of the sound, and approached warily. Having walked a short distance I reached the edge of the swamps, or rather a dry spot or oasis in the swamp, and by the faint glimmer of day, which was just breaking, I could see the outlines of a house. The cock continued to crow, which seemed to invite me to approach, and which I construed into a good omen,--at least I really felt good at the sight of the house, even though it might contain those who would chain me and take me back to my master. I noticed that a public road ran along close to the house; and after going on the road, in approaching the house I was discovered by a dog, belonging to the house, who set up a furious barking. Fearing to stay and make my wants known I again sought "cover" in the swamp. I stayed in the swamp that day and ate such berries, roots, and nuts as I could find. I had plenty of time for prayer and meditation. I was alone with God, and prayed to him for help in my distress, and for direction. I became convinced that I had done wrong in running away, and deemed that I had sinned against God. I had been a runaway and an outcast before, and had came to right conclusions; yet I had turned from the path of duty, and was even now being punished for my sin. I determined to return to my master and take the consequences of my acts in running away. I asked God to have mercy on me and pardon my sins, and protect me from the wrath of my master and the maliciousness of Hines. Having fully made up my mind to return to

Thompson and make such efforts as I could to allay the punishment I expected to receive, I set about perfecting my plans to get there without being apprehended by the slave-hunters, who were then, I have no doubt, hunting for me. My master had offered a reward for my return to his plantation; and should anyone arrest me and take me home, although I might be returning on my own accord, they would receive the reward and I would have to make up the amount to my master in extra labor and extra punishment. To avoid this was now my object.

At night, I left the swamp and went to the road, intending to travel home that night-- thinking I was not more than ten or twelve miles away from there. I was uncertain which way to go; but I finally started off on the road, hoping that I was going in the direction of Thompson's. The rain was pattering down; but I traveled briskly all that night, and about daybreak I came to a plantation. I entered one of the slave-cabins and told the inmates I was lost, hungry, and tired, and asked them for something to eat. One of the colored men spoke to a woman who appeared to be his wife, and told her to get me something to eat, and that he would go and get some pine to put on the fire. His actions, and the manner in which he spoke, aroused my suspicions, and being fearful that he intended to betray me, I left the cabin directly after he did, and sought an asylum in the woods, where I stayed during that day. Thus "the wicked flee when no one pursueth."

At night, I found the same road I had traveled the day before, and started again to try and get to Thompson's. I knew that I was wrong, and that I was traveling away from instead of toward Thompson's; therefore I concluded to make inquiries at the first opportunity. After traveling three or four miles I came to a cabin in which there was a light shining through the cracks between the logs. Approaching the cabin, I intended to enter; but being enabled to see the inmates through the cracks, I discovered three white men sitting around the fire, so I turned to leave. As I was passing the corner of the cabin, a colored woman came to the door for some purpose, and saw me. She jumped back into the cabin, at the same time exclaiming, "Here's a runaway nigger!"

I immediately ran for the road; but a dog--not a blood-hound--followed me, and while getting over the fence between the cabin and the road he caught me by the breeches leg. I shook him off and ran for the woods.

The white men were slave-hunters, and were after me particularly, as I learned afterwards. They followed me closely by the sound of the crackling of brush, and put the dogs they had with them on my track. These dogs, fortunately for me, were in the cabin at the time I approached it. As soon as I heard the first yelp of a bloodhound I "smutted" my shoe-soles, and soon threw them off the scent. The white men followed me about three or four miles. Finally, finding I would not get away from them by running, I stopped, and making my way into a dense thicket of briers I sat down. The white men stopped a short distance from me and listened, I suppose, for the sound of brush cracking. After waiting a short time one of them started off in the direction they had come, leaving the others still waiting,--using this ruse in order to throw me off my guard, so as to enable the remaining ones to ascertain where I was by the noise I would make in walking. I was too close to them; and from the noise I heard from where they were standing I knew they had a dog with them, and, that they were only waiting for me to move to begin the chase again. I sat perfectly quiet, and waited patiently for the remaining whites and the dog to leave. After a time the men began to move about through the brush, coming still closer to me. I heard them talking, when one of them said, "We ought to catch the nigger if we have to run him all night." "No," said the other, "we should let him alone to-night, and start him up in the morning, when we can have daylight for the chase, and not run him to-night, for we might run him off and never catch him."

After a short parley they concluded to get some more dogs and be on the ground before daylight, so as to make sure of me. As soon as they had gone out of my hearing I emerged from the brier thicket. I found my limbs had become sore and benumbed from the exposure and hardships I had undergone, and I was intensely hungry. I worried along, however, to get out of that neighborhood as soon as possible. The sky was now clear, the air frosty, and my rags were but a scant protection to me. After walking awhile I found my soreness began to leave me, when I began to accelerate my pace. I had to walk as fast as I could, and exercise my limbs all I could, in order to keep warm. After walking some time, I came to a plantation. Upon reconnoitering, I found an old house, and approaching it with the intention of seeking a little rest in it during the remainder of the night and the next day, I saw a light in it. I went in, however, and found it to be the workshop of the plantation, and five colored men were there putting handles in their axes. I asked them for something to eat, and was about to tell them the truth regarding myself, when one of the negroes hurried me out of the cabin, saying he would get me something to eat. After we got out he told me I was very imprudent, for if I had told the negroes who I was and that I was a runaway, they would have taken me themselves. He got me some meat and bread, and after I had told him who I was and that I wanted to find, my way back to Thompson's, he put me on the right road and gave me such directions, as I required.

I found that I was about fifty miles from Thompson's plantation, and that it would require two nights' hard walking to get there. I felt very much discouraged, and grieved considerably to myself. However, having satisfied the cravings of my appetite, I plucked up courage and started on my long return walk with renewed energy.

After traveling about five miles, I came to a little town. I was afraid to go through it on account of the liability of being apprehended; and I did not like to go around it for fear of getting lost again. I determined to risk going through the place, and, by avoiding every one, escape detection. There was quite an excitement here by reason of an epidemic sickness among the children, and about every other house had a light in it. I passed through the town with fear; but I escaped arrest and felt like rejoicing over my good fortune, not once thinking of any dangers or hardships that might lay before me.

After I got through the town, I came to a considerable stream, with a bridge across it, the name of which I am unable to give; but on the opposite end of the bridge from the town there is a road-way, or levee, thrown up across the "bottom" for about two miles. At the time I crossed, the stream was very much swelled from the recent rains, and the water extended all over the bottom on each side of the road-grade, and to within two or three feet of the top of it. This grade I had to cross; and I was greatly afraid that I would meet someone. I started across, and when about half way over the grade, or levee, I heard hounds baying ahead of me; and the sounds seemed to be approaching me. I became very much frightened, and turned and fled back to the bridge, when, just as I was stepping on it, I heard men's voices, and stopped, when I found they were coming across the bridge toward me. I concluded I would rather face the bloodhounds than the white men, so I made my way back over the grade as hurriedly as I could. I reached the end of the grade without meeting the hounds and turned off into the woods. After walking a short distance, I heard the hounds again, and the sound of their yelps was nearing me rapidly. I turned my course immediately, and ran as fast as I was able for three or four hundred yards, when I saw distinctly, in the starlight, a man running nearly toward me. My heart leaped into my throat, as it were, and I made ready for battle. But the man proved to be a poor runaway like myself, and the one whom the hounds were after. I had got into a field, and the runaway passed through the same field without noticing me. I kept on in an opposite direction from the one which he had taken, and crossed the fence on the other side of the field just in time to hear one of the slave-hunters say, "There he is now; I heard him getting over the fence." I threw myself on the ground and awaited results. The dogs were "hot" on the other slave's track, and were running at a great rate, which induced the slave-hunters to think their companion was mistaken. So, to my great relief and pleasure, they started on after the hounds. I was nearly exhausted by my exertions during the night, and as it was now nearly morning I lay on the ground for a time to rest and recuperate my worn-out energies a little.

In a short time, I got up, and after looking around, I saw the outlines of plantation houses in the distance. On going to them I found a resting-place in a fodder-loft, in the horse-lot of the plantation. I ensconced myself in the fodder, when I again heard the infernal yelps of the bloodhounds, and the more infernal yelps of the white pursuers urging the hounds after the poor runaway. The hounds soon after caught the poor wretch, whose cries for mercy were heart-rending and piteous. My situation was perilous; yet I had hopes that the other slave being run down and caught would save me, from the fact that the hunters were not aware of the presence of another runaway in the immediate neighborhood.

The day wore slowly away, and being very weak from hunger and fatigue I was unable to gain that rest my wasted body required. I slept two or three hours, however, and had ample time for reflection. The bridge where I had been so completely hemmed in the night before was impressed deeply upon my memory; and the agony of mind while on the bridge was still troubling me. I relied on a loving heavenly Father in my troubles and trials, and brought to my mind the condition of the children of Israel when about to be overwhelmed by the hosts of Pharaoh on the shore of the Red Sea. God delivered them, and I believed he would deliver me. My faith was strong.

Night came at last, when I cautiously emerged from my hiding-place and continued my journey toward home. I ran and walked about twenty-five miles, and did not find any familiar objects to lead me to suppose I was in the neighborhood of my master's plantation, when I began to look about for a place of concealment in which to spend another weary and lonesome day. Walking slowly along, after a short time my attention was attracted by sounds as if someone was pounding a hard substance. On stopping and listening, I soon heard some person calling hogs. The voice seemed familiar. Upon further investigation, I began to recognize objects, and soon ascertained that I was "at home." Now that I had got back "home," new troubles arose in my mind. I would be punished severely, without doubt.

Instead of going to "the quarters", I went directly to my master's plantation, in the hope that I could enlist my mistress in my behalf, and thus have the way made smooth for me. My master was not at home, fortunately, and my mistress heard my story and prayers for forgiveness. She promised to intercede with my master for me, but that I must promise not to run away again, which I did. She bade me to go and hide myself in the stable loft, and not to leave there until she sent for me. Soon after, my master came home. In conversation with him my mistress broached the subject as to my whereabouts. He told her that he believed I had got to the free states and was lost to him; however, that if any of the slaves on the plantation knew where I was they should get me word that if I would come back I should not be punished, and that I should be forgiven. In that case my mistress said she would insure my return speedily.

Matters were soon arranged, and I was re-instated in my former position on the plantation. But severe trials were soon to overtake me, and what I had already gone through was but an atom in comparison with what I afterwards suffered from the hands of my master, and by reason of my condition of slavery.

Thus ended my earlier experiences as a slave, from my earliest recollection down to the time of my return to Thompson's plantation.

I propose to continue this biography, and include the whole in book form. This pamphlet is printed for the purpose of enabling me to raise money to continue my work and paying for printing the whole in a book substantially and neatly bound.

To the friends of the colored race I appeal for help in this matter, hoping that sufficient interest is taken to insure the accumulation of sufficient funds for my purpose.

The remainder will contain my full experience as a minister of the gospel, and incidents relating to my efforts and the efforts of my co-workers in building up the church of Christ among the former slaves of the South, and such suggestions as I may deem proper to aid to raise the standard of intelligence among negroes.

Biography of a Slave

www.ingramcontent.com/pod-product-compliance
Lightning Source LLC
Chambersburg PA
CBHW070120100426
42744CB00010B/1883